Arbor Medicinae

Arbor Medicinae
The Tree of Medicine

**Eshaan Vasudev, Krish Vasudev,
Ronald D. Roessler, MD**

Illustrated by Aida El-Hajjar

Henschel
HAUS
www.henschelHAUSbooks.com
Milwaukee, Wisconsin

Published by
HenschelHAUS Publishing, Inc.
Milwaukee, Wisconsin
www.henschelHAUSbooks.com

ISBN: 979-8-9921070-4-3
CIP: Pending

First printing: January 2025
Quantity discounts are available for non-profit and academic organizations. Please contact info@henschelHAUSbooks.com

Book design and layout by Eshaan Vasudev.
Illustrations by Aida El-Hajjar.

Printed in the United States of America

Fifty percent of the proceeds from the sale of this book will be donated to Wisconsin Junior Classical League (WJCL), National Junior Classical League (NJCL) and to promote Latin education.

TABLE OF CONTENTS

Preface

In an era of rapid medical advancements, understanding the Latin origins of medical terms builds a crucial foundation for students, healthcare professionals, and patients.

For students, this knowledge not only broadens their vocabularies but also enhances their analytical skills and their communication skills, essential for future academic and professional success. For patients, learning medical terminology provides a first step to understanding complex, and often scary health conditions.

This book aims to be a valuable starting resource for anyone who wants to learn more about the roots at the base of our ever-growing "tree of medicine," including aspiring physicians, students, researchers, classical scholars, patients, and curious people in general.

Skeletal System

The skeletal system provides structural support, protection for internal organs, and enables movement through its connection with the muscular system. It also plays a crucial role in blood cell production and mineral storage.

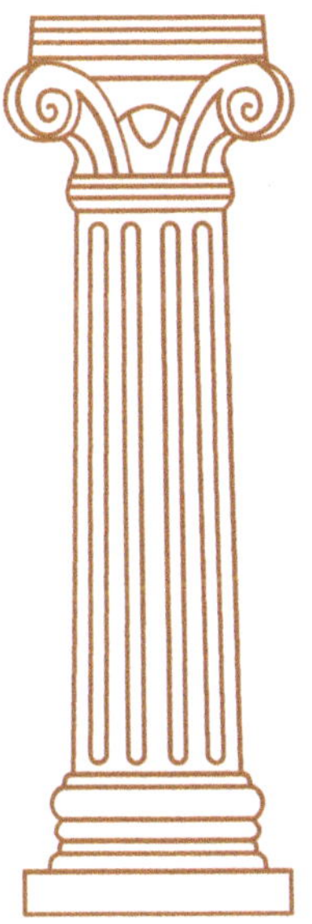

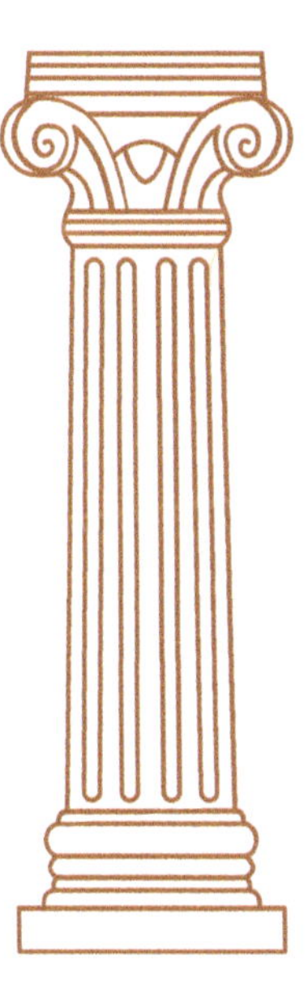

Examples

1. Femur

2. Metacarpals

3. Ligaments

4. Cartilage

Articulation

artus - joint

the connection between bones, allowing for movement and stability

Calcaneus

calx - heel

the heel bone

Carpal

carpus - wrist

Relating to the bones of the wrist

Cartilage

cartilago - cartilage, gristle

a soft, flexible tissue in the body that cushions joints

Cervical

cervix - neck

relating to the neck, specifically the vertebrae in the neck

Other Related Terms
article (*artus*)
calciform (*calx*)
metacarpal (*carpus*)
cervicovesical (*cervix*)
cervix (*cervix*)

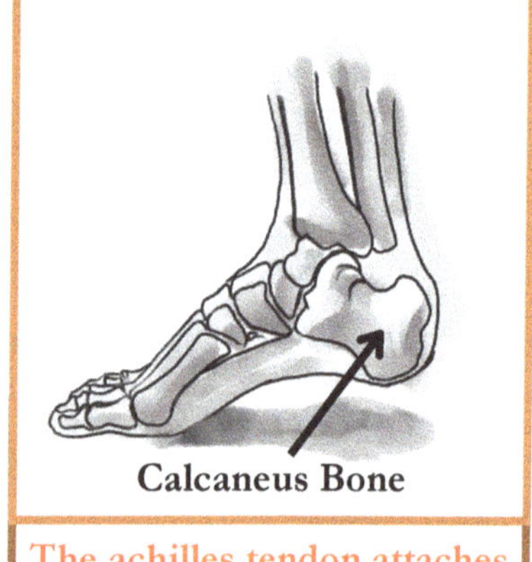

The achilles tendon attaches to the calcaneus.

Clavicle

clavis - key, bolt

the collar bone, linking the sternum and scapula

Cranium

cranium - skull

the part of the skull that encloses the brain

Fibula

fibula - clasp, brooch, peg, pin

a long thin bone in the lower leg; parallel to the tibia

Humerus

umerus - shoulder

the upper arm bone

Ilium

ilium - flank

the broad upper part of the hip bone

Other Related Terms

close (*clavis*)

disclose (*clavis*)

fixture (*fibula*)

prefix (*fibula*)

jade (*ilium*)

The cranium is made up of 8 bones.

Joint

iunctus -united, connected, associated

a structure where two bones meet

Lumbar

lumbus - loin

referring to the lower back or the lower part of the spine

Mandible

mandere - to chew

the lower jawbone

Marrow

medulla - marrow

soft fatty tissue inside bones that produce blood cells

Osseous

os - bone

made of bone or like bone

Other Related Terms

elumbated (*lumbus*)

manger (*mandere*)

masticate (*mandere*)

osprey (*os*)

ossicle (*os*)

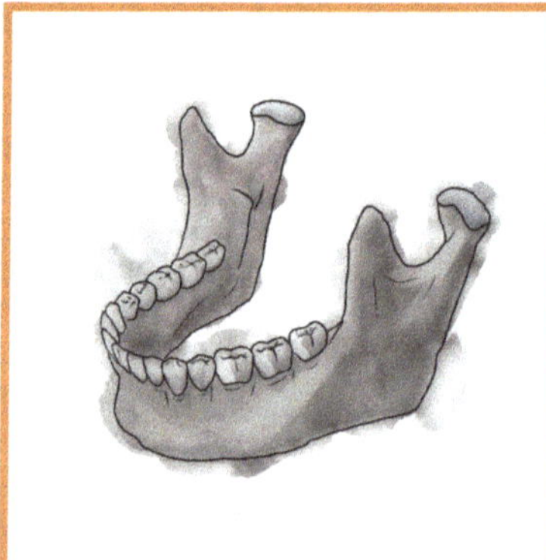

The mandible is the only bone in the skull that moves.

Ossification

os - bone + facere - to make

the process by which bones form

Patella

pateo - lie open

the kneecap bone

Pelvis

pelvis - basin, laver

the large bony structure near the base of the spine where the legs are attached

Sacrum

sacer - holy, sacred

a shield-shaped bone at the base of the spine between the hip bones

Skeleton

sceletus - skeleton (From Greek skeleton)

the framework of bones that supports the body

Other Related Terms
patio (*pateo*)
patent (*pateo*)
sacrifice (*sacer*)
sacrilegious (*sacer*)
desecrate (*sacer*)

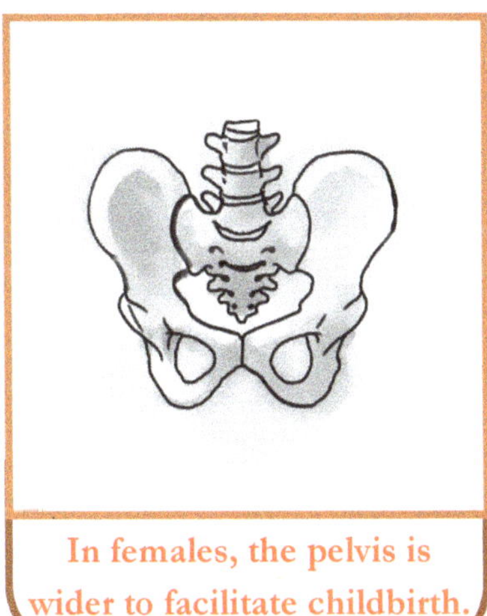

In females, the pelvis is wider to facilitate childbirth.

Spinal

spina - backbone, thorn

relating to the spine or backbone

Suture

suere - to sew

a means to hold body tissue together after an injury or surgery, also referred to as a stitch

Talus

talus - heel

the ankle bone that connects to the lower leg

Tibia

tibia - shinbone, pipe, flute

the larger bone in the lower leg, also referred to as the shinbone

Vertebra

vertere - to turn

a bone in the spinal column

Other Related Terms

spiny (*spina*)

sew (*suere*)

talon (*talus*)

vertical (*vertere*)

vertex (*vertere*)

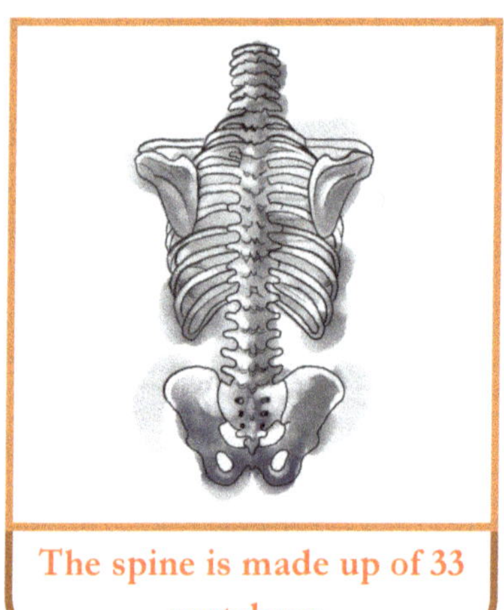

The spine is made up of 33 vertebrae.

In the spine, the first cervical vertebra is known as the atlas. This small bone supports the skull. The atlas vertebra allows the head to have a great amount of motion. The name for the atlas comes from Greek mythology: the story of the Titanomachy. Uranus was the god of the sky, and was married to Gaea, Mother Earth. Uranus despised his children, and locked them up in Tartarus. Upset about the treatment of her children, Gaea called upon her son, Cronus, to overthrow his father. With the help of his siblings, Cronus succeeded in castrating Uranus, thus freeing the imprisoned children.

After this event, Cronus took control of the universe, becoming the ruler of the gods. But as time passed, Cronus began to fear that his own children might one day rise up against him, just as he had done to his father. To prevent this, he swallowed each of his offspring upon its birth. However, his wife, Rhea, managed to save one child, Zeus, by tricking Cronus with a rock wrapped in swaddling clothes.

Zeus grew up in secret, eventually returning to confront his father. After a fierce battle known as the Titanomachy, Zeus and his allies, including his brothers Poseidon and Hades, defeated the Titans. Cronus was overthrown, and the reign of the Olympian gods began.

In the aftermath of the war, Zeus punished the Titans who had fought against him. Among them was Atlas, a powerful Titan who had sided with the enemy. As punishment for his role in the war, Zeus condemned Atlas to hold up the sky for eternity, just as the C1 vertebra, also called atlas, holds up the head.

Muscular System

The muscular system is an organ system that enables movement by contracting and relaxing muscles. It maintains posture, facilitates locomotion, and supports other bodily functions by generating force and aiding in blood flow and digestion. It also contributes to heat production.

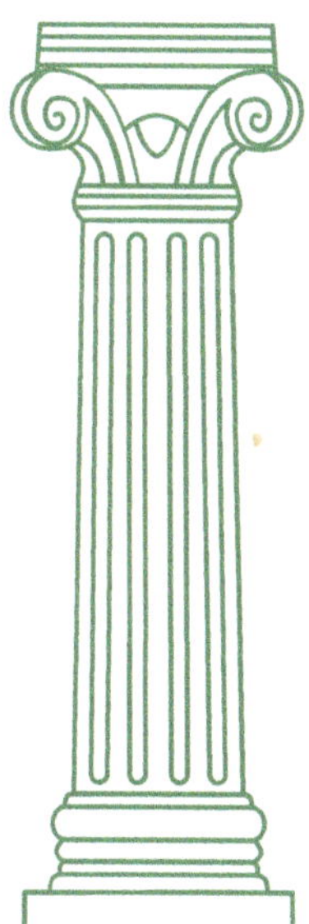

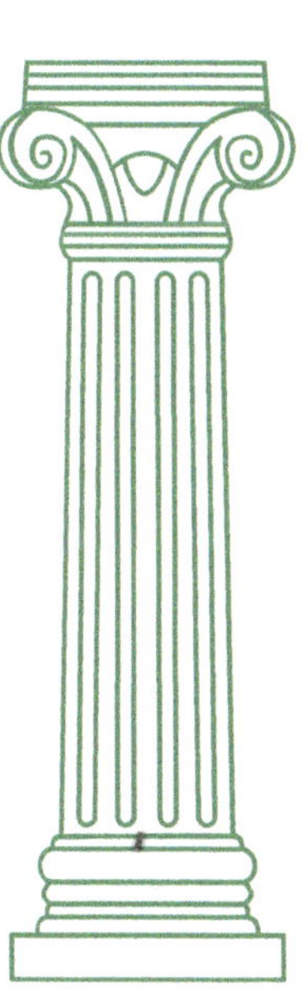

Examples

1. Biceps Femoris

2. Sternocleidomastoid

3. Tendons

4. Latissimus Dorsi

5. Masseter

Abductor

ab - away from + ducere - to lead

a muscle that moves a limb away from the body's midline

Adductor

ad - towards + ducere - to lead

a muscle that moves a limb toward the body's midline

Biceps

bi - two + caput - head

a muscle with two heads

Brachial

brachium - arm

pertaining to upper arm

Diaphragm

diaphragma - partition, (From Greek diaphragma)

a dome-shaped muscle that separates the thoracic and abdominal cavities

Other Related Terms

abduct (*ducere*)

conduct (*ducere*)

aqueduct (*ducere*)

chief (*caput*)

capital (*caput*)

The biceps are primarily responsible for flexing the elbow and rotating (supinating) the forearm.

Dorsal

dorsum - back

pertaining to the posterior side of the body

Extensor

extendere - to stretch out

a muscle that straightens a joint, increasing the angle between bones

Fiber

fibra - leaf, lobe

a single muscle cell which contracts to produce movement

Flexor

flectere - to bend

a muscle that bends a joint, decreasing the angle between bones

Gluteus

glutaeus - buttocks, the rump (From Greek gloutos)

three muscles in the buttocks responsible for movement of the hip and thigh

Other Related Terms
endorse (*dorsum*)
extend (*extendere*)
extensive (*extendere*)
defibrillator (*fibra*)
reflexive (*flextere*)

There are two types of muscle fibers: one with more endurance and the other with more power.

Muscular System

Latissimus

latissimus - widest

a large, broad muscle located on the back, known as the latissimus dorsi

Muscle

mus - mouse

a tissue capable of contracting to produce movement in parts of the body

Oblique

obliquus - slanting

muscles on the sides of the abdomen that assist in trunk rotation and lateral flexion

Pectoral

pectus - chest

pertaining to the chest muscles, primarily the pectoralis major and minor

Pronation

pronare - to bend forward

rotation of the forearm or foot that turns the palm downward or the sole inward

Other Related Terms

latitude (*latissimus*)

dilation (*latissimus*)

mouse (*mus*)

mussel (*mus*)

pecs (*pectoral*)

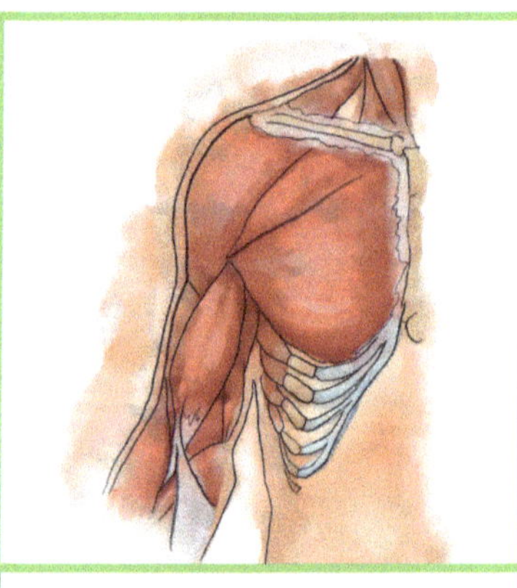

The pectoralis major brings the arms toward the body's midline (adduction) and rotates the arm inward.

Rectus

rectus - straight

a straight muscle, such as the rectus abdominis

Sacromere

sacro - flesh (From Greek sarx)

the basic unit of muscle contraction in striated muscle.

Soleus

solea - sole

a muscle in the calf that aids in plantar flexion of the foot

Spasm

spasmus - a spasm (From Greek spasmos)

an involuntary and sudden muscle contraction

Tendon

tendere - to stretch

a fibrous connective tissue that connects muscle to bone

Other Related Terms

correct (*rectus*)

sole (*soleus*)

tender (*tendere*)

tendency (*tendere*)

tent (*tendere*)

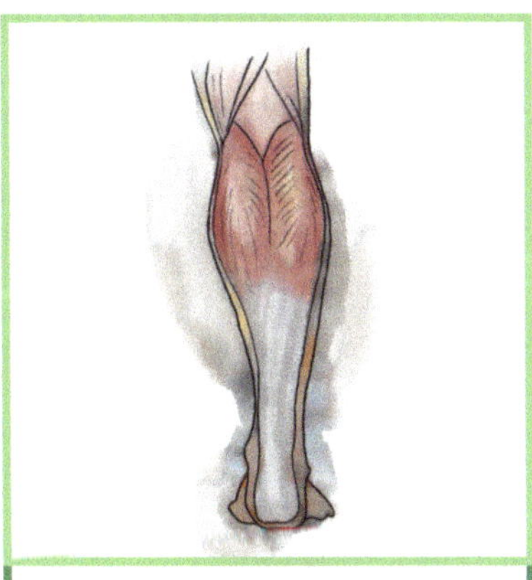

The achilles tendon is the strongest tendon in the body.

Teres

terere - to rub

shoulder muscles that help rotate and move the arm

Tetanus

tetanus - muscular spasm (From Greek tetanos)

a state of continuous muscle contractions

Torso

thyrsus - stalk, stem (From Greek thyrsos)

the main part of the body that contains the major muscle groups of the chest, back, and abdomen

Vastus

vastus - huge

muscles in the quadriceps group that are crucial for extending the knee

Zygomatic

zygomaticus - pertaining to the zygoma (From Greek zygoma)

facial muscles attached to the zygomatic bone

Other Related Terms

extort (*thyrsus*)

torque (*thyrsus*)

tortoise (*thyrsus*)

vast (*vastus*)

waste (*vastus*)

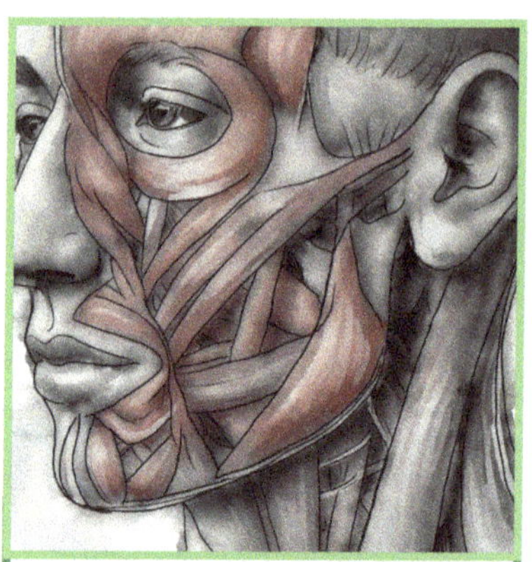

The zygomaticus major raises the corners of the mouth, which is essential for facial expressions.

The achilles tendon connects the calf muscles to the heel bone, allowing the foot to push off the ground and propel the body forward when walking, running, or jumping. Despite its strength, the achilles tendon is named for its weakness, and how it led to the downfall of the mythical warrior Achilles. Born to the sea-nymph Thetis and the mortal king Peleus, Achilles was dipped into the River Styx as an infant, making his body impervious to harm. However, his mother held him by his heel, leaving that one small spot untouched by the magical waters. Achilles became the most feared warrior in the Trojan War, celebrated for his strength and speed. His near invulnerability allowed him to charge fearlessly into battle, knowing that he could not be harmed by weapons or blows. He defeated foe after foe, but all it took was one arrow, shot by Paris of Troy and guided by the god Apollo, which hit him in the heel and his Achilles tendon to put an end to his supremacy.

Today, the term "Achilles' heel" has come to symbolize any singular vulnerability in an otherwise strong or invincible person or thing, and this tendon in the human body reflects him and his eventual demise.

Integumentary System

The integumentary system is the body's outer protective layer, consisting primarily of the skin, hair, nails, and associated glands. It acts as a barrier against environmental hazards, regulates temperature, and provides sensory information.

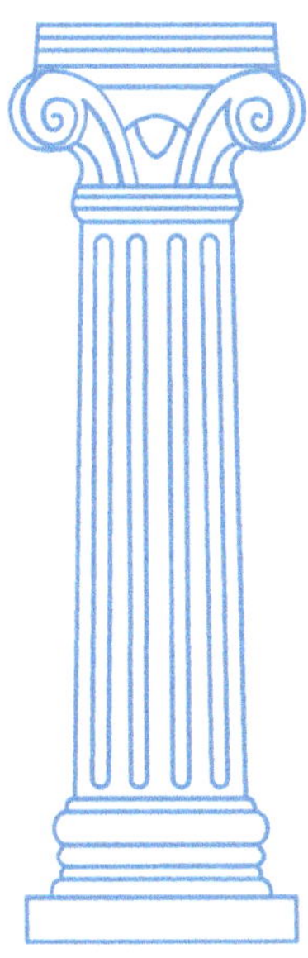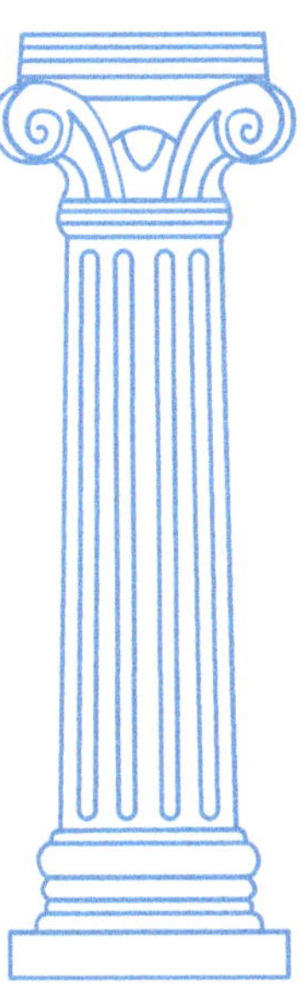

Examples

1. Epidermis

2. Dermis

3. Hair follicles

4. Sebaceous (oil) glands

5. Sweat glands

Albinism
albus - white

a condition that leads to an individual having white or very light skin, hair, and eyes

Callus
callum - hard, thick skin

an area of hard, thickened skin most often on the hands or feet

Collagen
colla - glue (From Greek kolla)

primary protein in connective tissue

Contusion
tundere - to beat, strike

a bruise

Cutaneous
cutis - skin

relating to the skin

Other Related Terms
albino (*albus*)
callosity (*callum*)
protocol (*colla*)
obtunded (*tundere*)
cuticle (*cutis*)

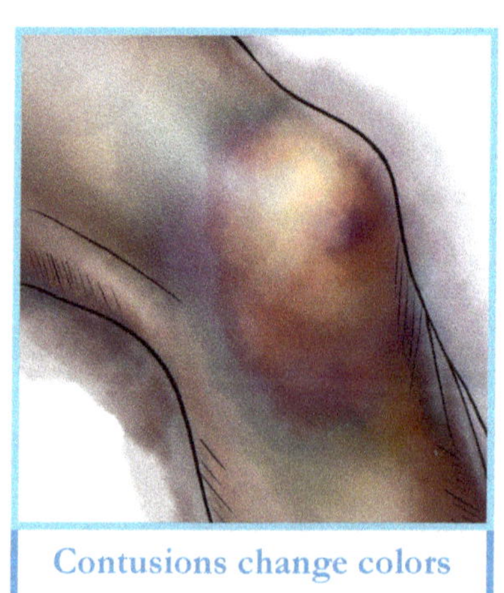

Contusions change colors over time.

Integumentary System

Dermatologist

derma - skin, leather (From Greek derma)

doctor who specializes in treating the skin, hair, and nails

Edema

oedema - a swelling (From Greek oidema)

swelling caused by trapped fluid in tissue

Erythema

erythema - a redness on the skin (From Greek erythema)

redness of the skin

Follicle

follis - bag, sac

a small cavity, sac, or gland that may secrete a chemical or contain a structure inside

Gangrene

gangraena - an eating or gnawing sore (Latinized from the Greek gangraina)

tissue that has died due to an infection or a lack of blood supply

Other Related Terms

dermabrasion (*derma*)

epidermis (*derma*)

taxidermy (*derma*)

foolish (*follis*)

foolproof (*follis*)

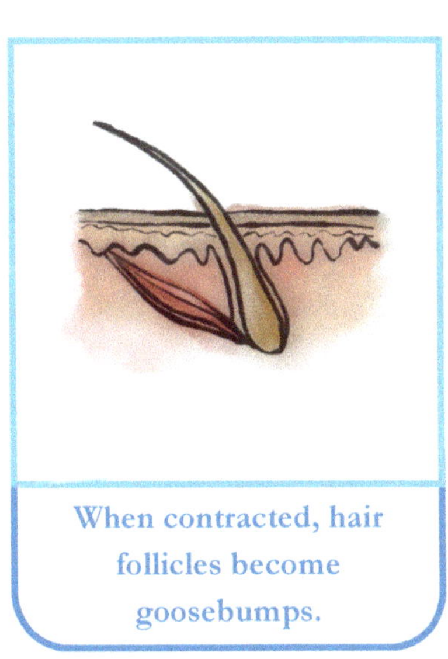

When contracted, hair follicles become goosebumps.

Impetigo

impetus - an attack

a very contagious skin infection common among children

Incision

caedere - to cut

a cut made into skin/flesh

Inflammation

flamma - flame

body's response to injury and invasion in order to protect itself

Laceration

lacer - torn into pieces, mangled

a deep tear in the flesh or skin

Lesion

laedere - to strike, hurt, injure

a region in a tissue or organ that has been hurt or damaged

Other Related Terms

incompetent (*impetus*)
indecisive (*caedere*)
scissor (*caedere*)
flambe (*flamma*)
collide (*laedere*)

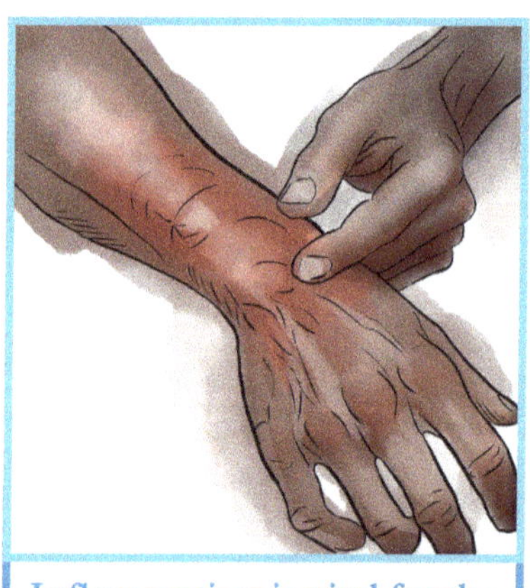

Inflammation is vital for the body's immune response.

Melanin

melas - a black spot on the skin (From Greek melas)

a pigment that plays a major role in the color of skin, eyes, and hair

Nodule

nodus - knot

a small, knot-like growth under the skin

Papule

papula - pimple, swelling

a rounded lump or small area of swelling in the body

Pruritus

prurire - to itch

itching; a sensation on the skin that makes you want to scratch

Rash

rasus - scraped

a portion of skin that is changed in color and texture

Other Related Terms
melanoma (*melas*)
noose (*nodus*)
papillary (*papule*)
pruritic (*prurire*)
erase (*rasus*)

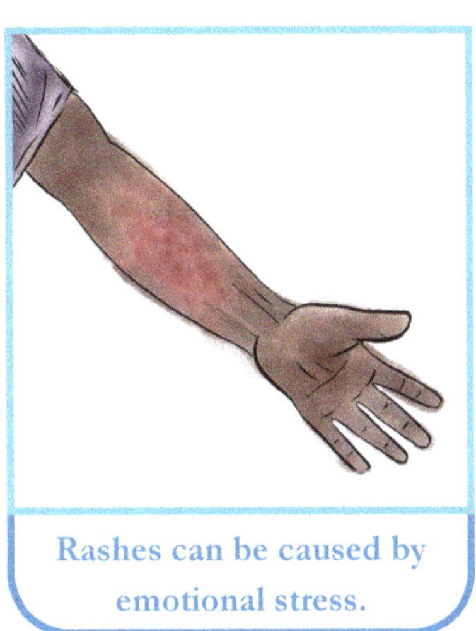

Rashes can be caused by emotional stress.

Scar

eschara - scar (From Greek eskhara)

a mark on the skin caused by an injury not completely healing

Sebaceous

sebum - tallow, grease

similar to fat or grease

Ulcer

ulcus - a sore (From Greek elkos)

an internal or external sore

Varicose

varix - dilated vein

describes a vein that is enlarged, twisted, or bulging

Vitiligo

vitiligo - a kind of cutaneous eruption, blemish

a chronic disorder that causes areas of the skin to lose color

Other Related Terms
eschar (*eschara*)
vice (*eschara*)
sebotrophic (*sebum*)
sebum (*sebum*)
ulcerate (*ulcus*)

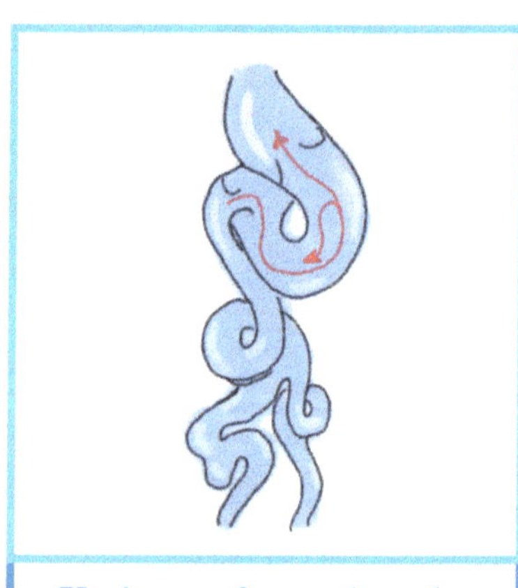

Varicoses form when the valves inside veins fail, causing blood to pool.

The skin, the body's largest organ, is both a protective shield and a symbol of resilience, illustrated in the myth of Hercules and the Nemean lion.

As one of his Twelve Labors, Hercules was sent to slay the Nemean lion, a ferocious beast directed by Hera to terrorize the region of Nemea. The lion's hide was said to be impenetrable, rendering all weapons useless. Faced with an opponent that could not be harmed by conventional means, Hercules relied on his wits and raw power. He pursued the lion into its lair, blocked one of the cave's two entrances to prevent its escape, and engaged it in close combat. After a brutal struggle, Hercules used his strength to strangle the lion to death. Afterwards, he cleverly used the lion's own razor-sharp claws to skin the beast. Hercules crafted the hide into a cloak, wearing it as both armor and a sign of his triumph.

The story of the Nemean lion's skin persisted throughout time, influencing figures like the Roman Emperor Caligula. Obsessed with power and desperate to be seen as a living god, Caligula adorned himself with a lion-skin cloak, imitating Hercules' iconic look. While the cloak might have evoked the imagery of heroism, Caligula lacked the deeds to back it up, and his violent and cruel actions overshadowed his image.

The Nemean lion's skin, like the human skin, is shaped by what is endured, and serves as a barrier between not only ourselves and our environment, but also strength and vulnerability.

Nervous System

The nervous system controls and coordinates bodily functions and responses to internal and external stimuli through a network of neurons and supporting cells.

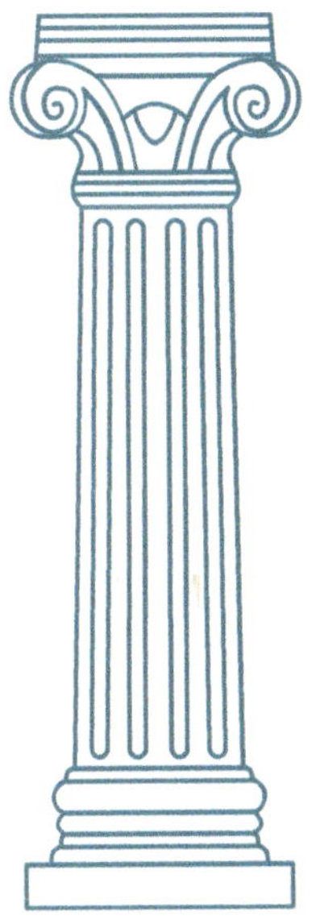

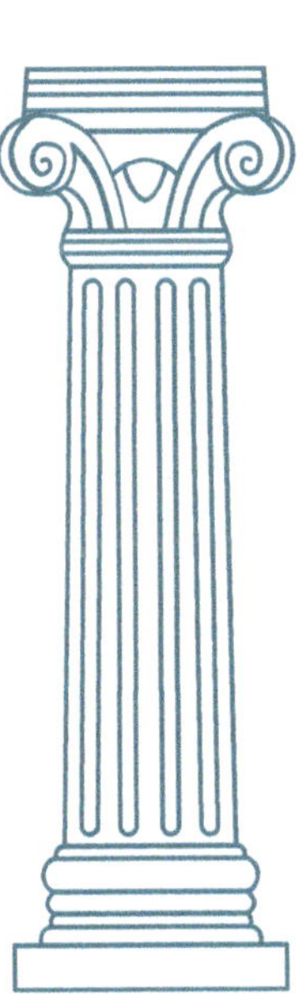

Examples

1. Cauda Equina

2. Corpus Callosum

3. Sciatic Nerve

4. Frontal Lobe

5. Spinal Cord

Accumbens

accumbere - to recline or lie down

refers to the nucleus accumbens, a brain region involved in reward and pleasure

Afferent

afferre - to carry towards

nerve fibers carrying sensory signals to the central nervous system

Brain

cerebrum - brain

the central organ that processes sensory information and controls bodily functions

Cauda Equina

cauda - horse + equus - tail

a bundle of spinal nerves at the lower end of the spinal cord

Corpus Callosum

corpus - body + callus - tough

a thick band of nerve fibers that facilitates communication between the two hemispheres of the brain

Other Related Terms

aquifer (*afferre*)

confer (*afferre*)

cerebellum (*cerebrum*)

coward (*cauda*)

equestrian (*equus*)

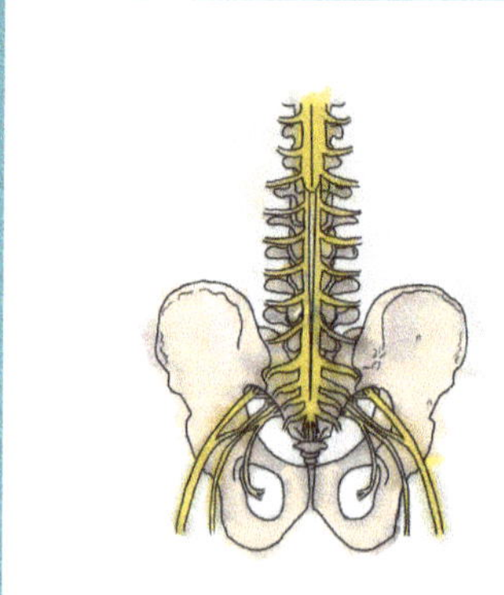

The cauda equina contains nerves which control the lower limbs and bladder.

Efferent

efferre - to carry away

nerve fibers carrying signals from the central nervous system to the body

Glia

glia - glue (From Greek glia)

supportive cells in the nervous system that protect and nourish neurons

Hippocampus

hippocampus - seahorse (From Greek hippokampos)

a brain region, shaped like a fish, crucial for memory and learning

Impulse

impellere - to strike against

a sudden, rapid electrical signal that travels along a nerve fiber

Limbic

limbus - edge

relating to the limbic system, a complex system of brain structures involved in emotions, behavior, and memory

Other Related Terms

difference (*efferre*)

deferral (*efferre*)

expel (*impellere*)

propel (*impellere*)

push (*impellere*)

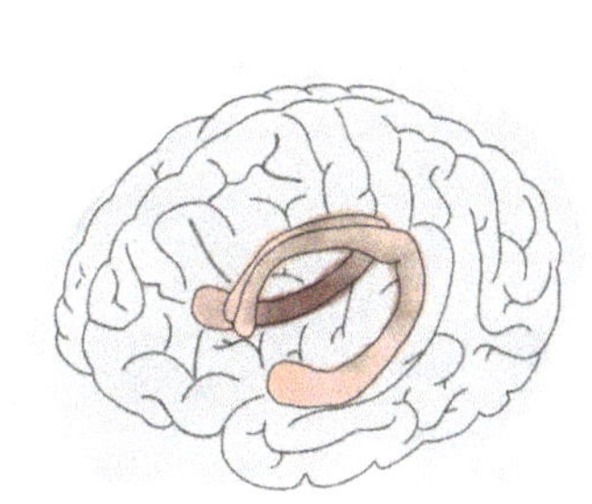

Degeneration of the hippocampus is a hallmark of Alzheimer's disease, leading to memory loss.

Lobe

lobus - hull, pod (From Greek lobos)

a division of the brain responsible for certain functions

Meninges

meninx - membrane (From Greek meninx)

protective membranes surrounding the brain and spinal cord

Motor

movere - to move

relating to movement control by the nervous system

Nucleus

nucleus - kernel

the kernel, inner part, or inside of a thing

Occipital

ob - in the back of + caput - head

pertaining to the occipital lobe, which processes visual information

Other Related Terms

automobile (*movere*)

emotion (*movere*)

nucleic (*nucleus*)

captain (*caput*)

mischief (*caput*)

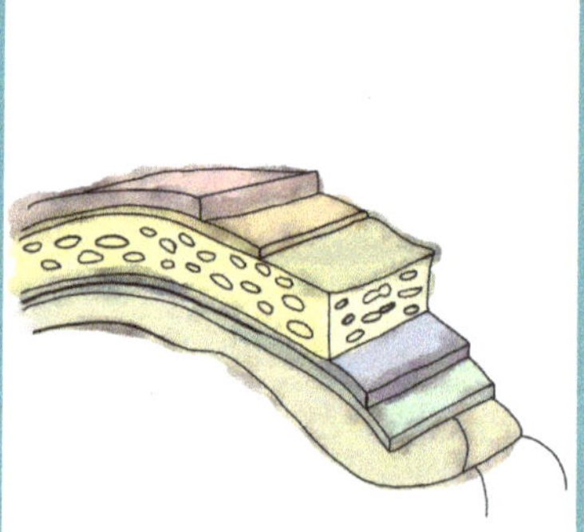

The inner layer of the meninges contains blood vessels that supply nutrients and oxygen to the brain and spinal cord.

Olfactory

olfacere - to get the smell of

relating to the sense of smell

Parietal

paries - wall

pertaining to the parietal lobe, which processes sensory information

Plexus

plectere - to twine, braid, fold

a network of intersecting nerves

Pons

pons - bridge

a bridge-like region of the brainstem involved in signaling and regulating vital functions

Receptor

recipere - to receive

a specialized cell or structure that responds to stimuli

Other Related Terms
magnify (*olfacere*)
ossification (*olfacere*)
duplicate (*plectere*)
imply (*plectere*)
recover (*recipere*)

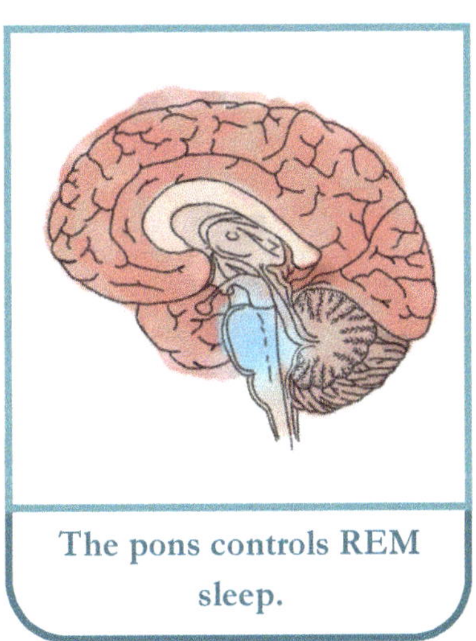

The pons controls REM sleep.

Nervous System

Reflex

reflectere - to bend back

an automatic response to a stimulus

Sensory

sentire - to perceive, feel

relating to the perception of stimuli through senses

Temporal

tempus - time, season

relating to the temporal lobe, which processes auditory information and memory, located near the temples where hair turns gray over time

Vagus

vagus - wandering, straying

a cranial nerve involved in controlling heart rate, digestion, and other autonomic functions that takes a long, wandering course from the brainstem to the abdominal organs

Visceral

viscus - internal organ/part of the body

relating to the nervous system's control of internal organs

Other Related Terms

flexible (*reflectere*)

consent (*sentire*)

nonsense (*sentire*)

temper (*tempus*)

extravagant (*vagus*)

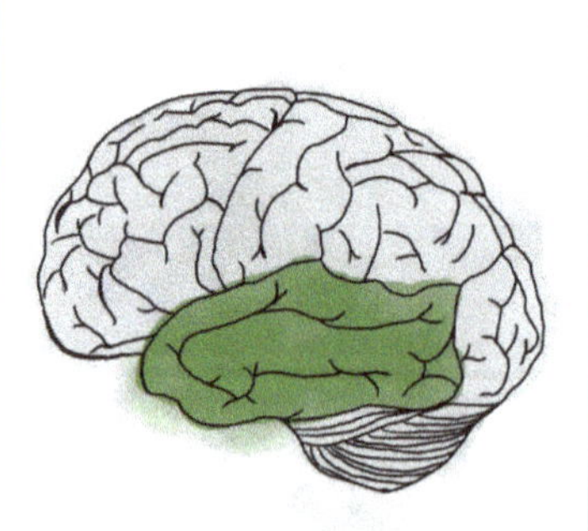

The left temporal lobe conatins Wernicke's area, which is critical for language comprehension.

The brain is the body's control center, responsible for thoughts, memory, emotions, and all voluntary and involuntary actions. However, above all, the brain is primarily known for giving us wisdom and intellect. This reputation of the brain has existed for thousands of years, as reflected in the origin of Athena, the goddess of wisdom.

Zeus, the king of the gods, swallowed his first wife, Metis, the goddess of wisdom and craft, fearing a prophecy that their child would be mightier than he. However, when the time came for the birth of their child, Zeus was struck by an excruciating headache. Unable to bear the pain, he ordered Hephaestus, the god of smithing, to split open his skull with an axe. From the cleft in Zeus's head sprang Athena, fully grown and clad in armor.

Athena's wisdom is also visible in her contest with Poseidon for patronage of a city. The citizens asked each deity to present a gift to determine the victor. Poseidon struck the earth with his trident, and a saltwater spring surged, symbolizing his power over the seas. Athena, however, offered something far more practical: an olive tree. She explained its myriad uses—wood for building, fruit for nourishment, and oil for light and trade. The citizens recognized her gift's value and chose Athena as their patron goddess, calling their city Athens.

Athena's origins from Zeus's head and her actions tie her directly to intellect and decision-making, much like how the brain is central to human thought and problem-solving every day.

Cardiovascular System

The cardiovascular system circulates blood throughout the body, delivering oxygen and nutrients to tissues and removing waste products. It consists of the heart, blood vessels, and blood.

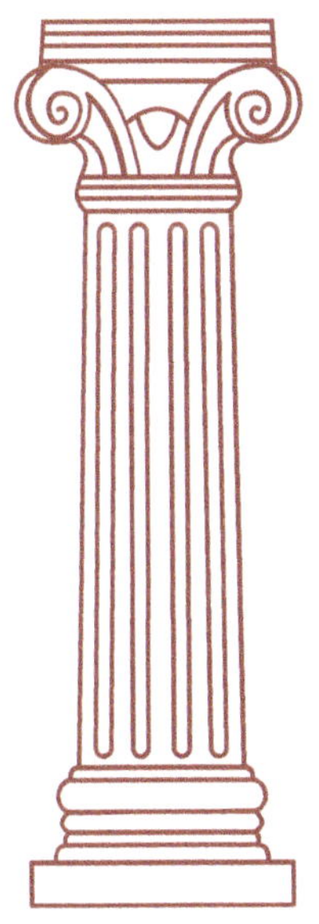

Examples

1. Mitral Valve

2. Right Ventricle

3. Aorta

4. Vena Cava

5. Left Atrium

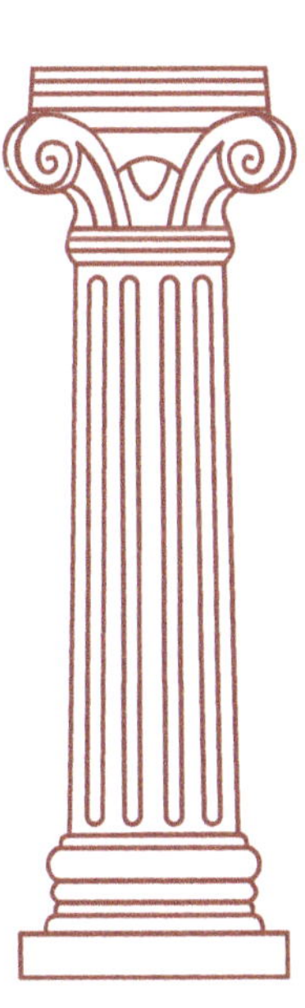

Angina (Pectoris)

angere - to strangle, suffocate

a feeling of tightness or suffocating pain in the chest

Atrium

atrium - first main room of a house

one of the two upper chambers of the heart

Capillary

capillus - hair

the smallest blood vessels where the exchange of oxygen, nutrients, and waste occurs between blood and tissues

Cardiac

cardiacus - pertaining to the heart (From Greek kardiakos)

relating to the heart

Circulation

circulus - circle, small ring

the movement of blood throughout the body, facilitated by the heart and blood vessels

Other Related Terms

angle (*angere*)

anguish (*angere*)

anxiety (*angere*)

chevelure (*capillus*)

disheveled (*capillus*)

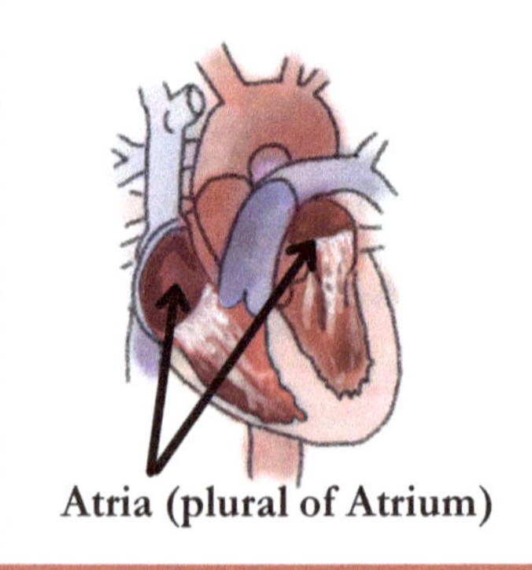

The left atrium holds oxygenated blood and the right atrium holds deoxygenated blood.

Coronary

corona - crown, wreath

pertaining to the arteries that supply blood to the heart muscle and encircle it like a crown

Fibrillation

fibra - leaf, lobe

rapid, irregular, and unsynchronized contraction of heart muscle fibers

Hypertension

hyper - over (Greek)+ tendere - to stretch

abnormally high blood pressure

Mitral

mitra - headband, turban, bishop's hat (17th century) (From Greek mitra)

the name of the "hat-shaped" valve which controls blood flow between the left atrium and left ventricle of the heart

Myocardium

myo - muscle + cor - heart

the muscular tissue of the heart

Other Related Terms
coronation (*corona*)
fiber (*fibra*)
tendon (*tendere*)
corageous (*cor*)
record (*cor*)

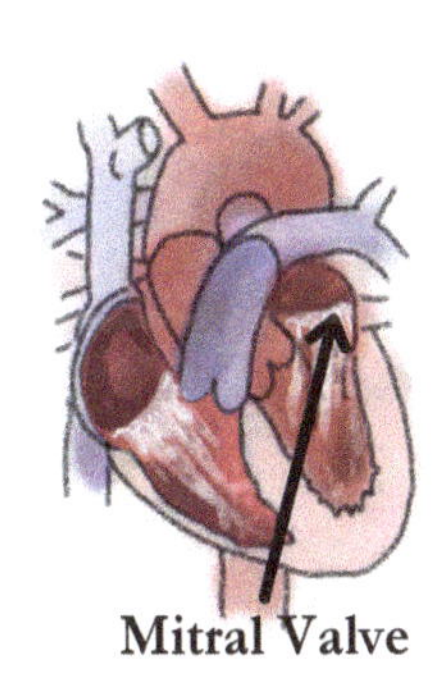

Mitral Valve

The mitral valve is the most frequently affected valve in heart diseases.

Occlusion

occludere - to close up

blockage or closing of a
blood vessel or hollow organ

Pacemaker

pax - peace

device or group of cells that
regulates the heartbeat

Palpitation

palpitare - to throb, flutter

noticeably rapid, strong,
fluttering, or irregular
heartbeat

Septum

saepes - hedge, fence

wall dividing two cavities,
such as the left and right
chambers of the heart

Stenosis

*stenosis - a narrowing (From
Greek stenos)*

abnormal narrowing of a
blood vessel or valve in the
heart

Other Related Terms
disclose (*occludere*)
recluse (*occludere*)
pacific (*pax*)
pact (*pax*)
palpable (*palpitare*)

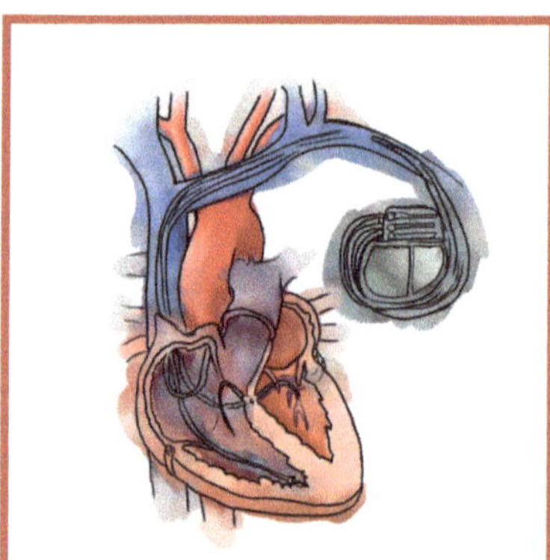

Pacemakers function for
around 10 years without
needing replacement.

Cardiovascular System

Tachycardia

tachy - swift + cor - heart

abnormally rapid heart rate

Tricuspid

tri - three + cuspis - point

relating to the tricuspid valve between the right atrium and right ventricle

Valve

valva - section of folding or revolving door

structure in the heart or veins that prevents the backward flow of blood

Vascular

vasculum - small vessel

relating to blood vessels

Vasoconstriction

vas - container + constringere - to bind together

narrowing of blood vessels by small muscles in their walls

Other Related Terms

accord (*cor*)

cusp (*cuspis*)

vase (*valva*)

vasectomy (*vas*)

vessel (*vas*)

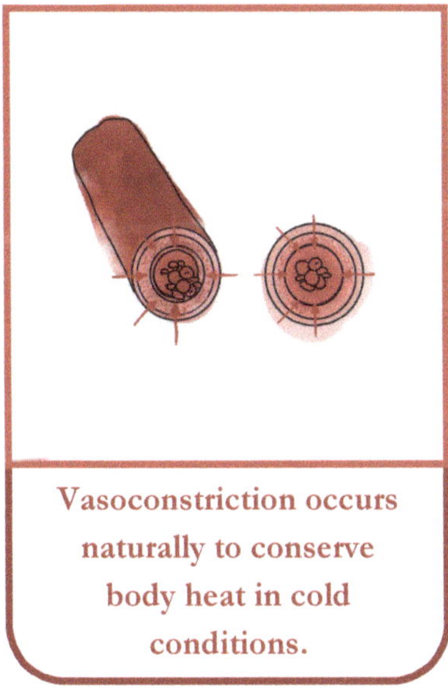

Vasoconstriction occurs naturally to conserve body heat in cold conditions.

Vasodilation

vas - container + dis - apart + latus - wide

widening of blood vessels resulting from relaxation of the muscular wall of the vessels

Vena Cava

vena - vein + cavus - hollow

one of the two large veins (superior and inferior) that carry deoxygenated blood to the heart

Venous

vena - vein

relating to veins

Ventricle

venter - belly

one of the two lower chambers of the heart

Vessel

vas - container

a tube through which blood flows in the body

Other Related Terms
latitude (*latus*)
cage (*cavus*)
excavator (*cavus*)
vein (*vena*)
ventral (*venter*)

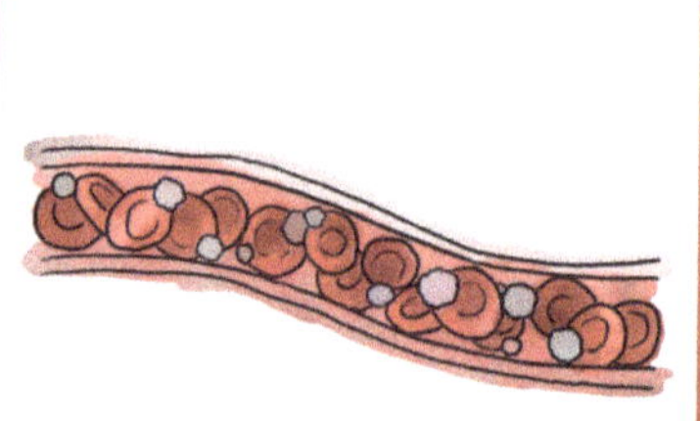

Arteries (vessels with oxygenated blood) have elastic walls to handle high-pressure blood flow from the heart.

Cupid, the god of love, used his arrows to strike the hearts of gods and mortals alike. He had two magical arrows: one tipped with gold, which inspired love, and the other tipped with lead, which caused disdain. Cupid shot his arrows at people's hearts, which were considered the seat of emotion and love.

One famous tale is that of Aeneas and Dido. Aeneas, a Trojan who fled from the Trojan war, was destined to found Rome, but along his journey, he stopped in Carthage, where Queen Dido welcomed him. Aphrodite, Aeneas' mother, worried that Hera, who hated Aeneas, might try and prevent him from fulfilling his fate and sent Cupid to ensure they fell in love. Disguised as Aeneas' son, Cupid shot the queen's heart with his golden arrow, filling her heart with an uncontrollable passion for Aeneas.

Dido, now overwhelmed by love, took Aeneas into her heart. But when Aeneas eventually had to leave to fulfill his destiny, Dido's heart was broken. She could not bear the pain of unrequited love, and in her sorrow, she took her own life.

Another famous tale is that of Apollo and Daphne. Apollo, the god of light and music, mocked Cupid's bow skills, claiming that his own archery was superior. Insulted, Cupid shot Apollo with his golden arrow, causing him to fall in love with Daphne, a nymph. Cupid then shot Daphne with his lead-tipped arrow, ensuring she would despise his love. As Apollo relentlessly pursued her, Daphne prayed to her father, the river god Peneus, to save her. In response, she was transformed into a laurel tree. The heartbroken Apollo vowed to honor her forever, making the laurel his sacred symbol.

Respiratory System

The respiratory system is a network of organs and tissues that facilitate the exchange of oxygen and carbon dioxide between the body and the environment, essential for breathing and cellular respiration.

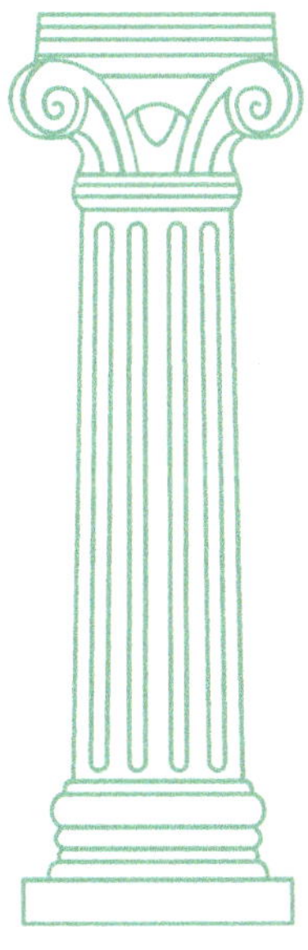

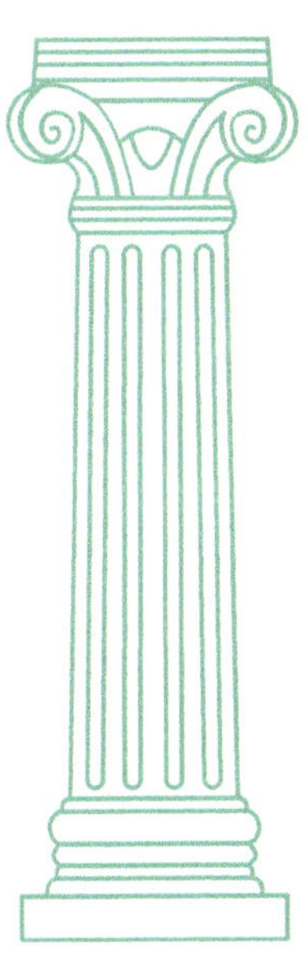

Examples

1. Cricoid Cartilage

2. Epiglottis

3. Lobes of the Lungs

4. Alveoli

5. Trachea

Alveolar

alveolus - socket, small cavity

relating to the tiny air sacs in the lungs where gas exchange occurs

Apnea

apnoea - absence of breath (From Greek apnoia)

temporary cessation of breathing

Bronchus

bronchus - wind pipe (From Greek bronkhos)

one of the two main branches of the trachea that lead into the lungs

Carbon

carbo - coal

a chemical element involved exhalation (carbon dioxide)

Cilia

cilium - upper eyelid

tiny hair-like structures that line the respiratory tract and help move mucus and debris out of the airways

Other Related Terms
bronchitis (*bronchus*)
carboxyl (*carbo*)
carbohydrate (*carbo*)
stereocilium (*cilium*)
supercilium (*cilium*)

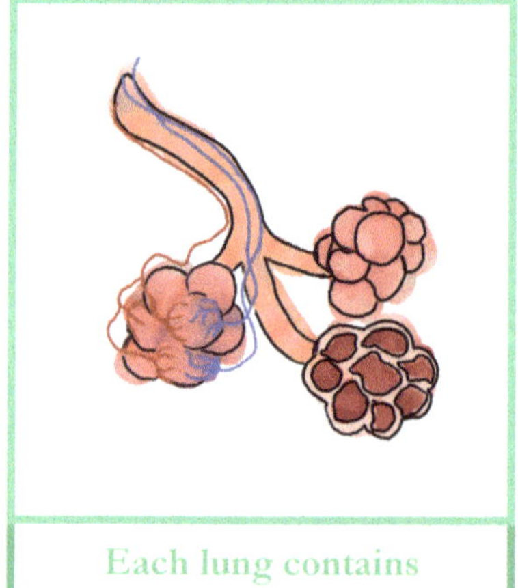

Each lung contains about 300 million alveoli.

Cisterna

cista - chest, box (From Greek kiste)

a reservoir or storage cavity in the respiratory system

Congestion

cum - with + gerere - to carry, bring, pile up

the accumulation of fluid in an organ or tissue

Cyanosis

cyanosis - dark blue color (From Greek kyanos)

a bluish discoloration of the skin due to lack of oxygen in the blood

Expiration

spirare - to breathe

the process of exhaling air from the lungs

Humidify

humidus - moist, wet + facere (to make)

to add moisture to the air, often to make it more suitable for breathing

Other Related Terms
digest (*gerere*)
gesture (*gerere*)
belligerent (*gerere*)
conspire (*spirare*)
spiritual (*spirare*)

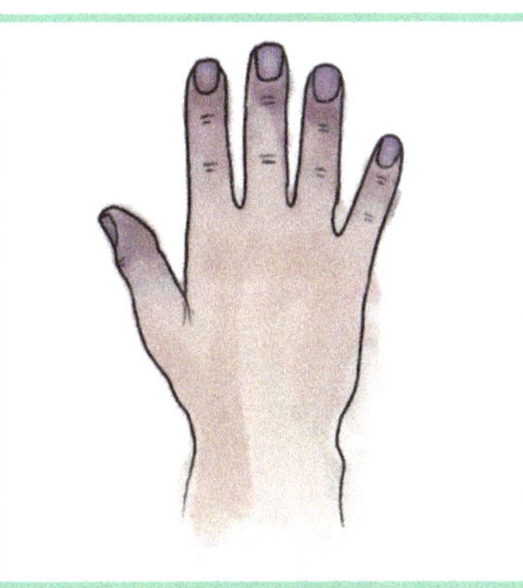

Cyanosis in the hands or feet is much less worrisome than cyanosis in the lips or tongue.

Respiratory System

Inhalation

inhalare - to breathe in

the process of breathing air into the lungs

Intercostal

inter - between + costa - rib

relating to the muscles located between the ribs

Larynx

larynx - upper windpipe (From Greek larynx)

the voice box located at the top of the trachea, involved in breathing, producing sound, and protection against food aspiration

Mucous

mucus - slimy, mucus

relating to the mucus produced by mucous membranes, which traps particles from the respiratory tract

Nasal

nasus - nose

relating to the nose and the nasal passages

Other Related Terms

coast (*costa*)

cutlet (*costa*)

moisture (*mucus*)

musty (*mucus*)

nares (*nasus*)

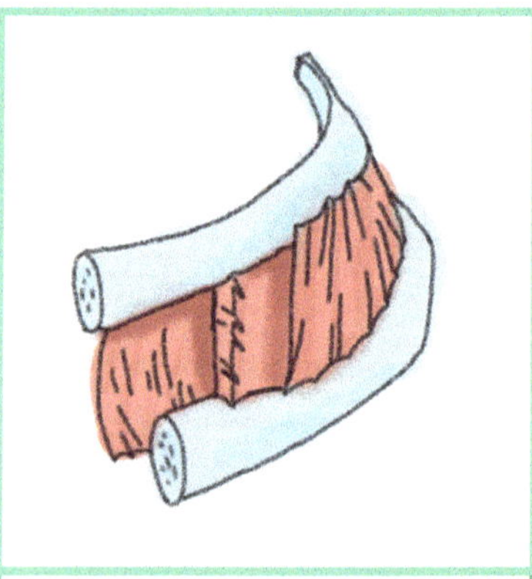

Singers rely on strong intercostal muscles to control air flow.

Respiratory System

Nebulizer

nebula - mist

a device that turns liquid medicine into a fine mist for inhalation, commonly used to treat asthma

Palate

palatum - roof of the mouth

the roof of the mouth, separating the oral and nasal cavities

Pleura

pleuron - rib, side (From Greek pleuron)

the membrane surrounding the lungs and lining the chest cavity, providing lubrication for lung movement

Pulmonary

pulmo - lung

relating to the lungs

Rhinitis

rhino - nose

inflammation of the nasal mucous membrane that causes a runny nose and congestion

Other Related Terms

nebula (*nebula*)
nebulous (*nebula*)
palatable (*palatum*)
pulmonology (*pulmo*)
rhinoceros (*rhino*)

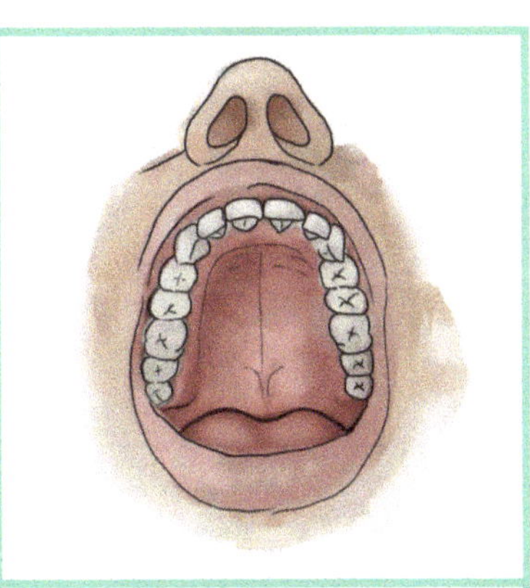

The palate contains taste receptors that help with tasting food.

Sinus

sinus - curve, fold

air-filled cavities within the skull that help lighten its weight and improve voice resonance

Sputum

spuere - to spit

mucus and other matter expelled from the lungs by coughing

Trachea

trachia - windpipe (From Greek trachkeia)

the windpipe, a tube that carries air from the larynx to the bronchi

Ventilation

ventus - wind

the process of moving air in and out of the lungs

Voice

vox - voice

the sound produced by the vibration of the vocal cords in the larynx

Other Related Terms

sine (*sinus*)
insinuate (*sinus*)
spew (*spuere*)
hyperventilate (*ventus*)
vent (*ventus*)

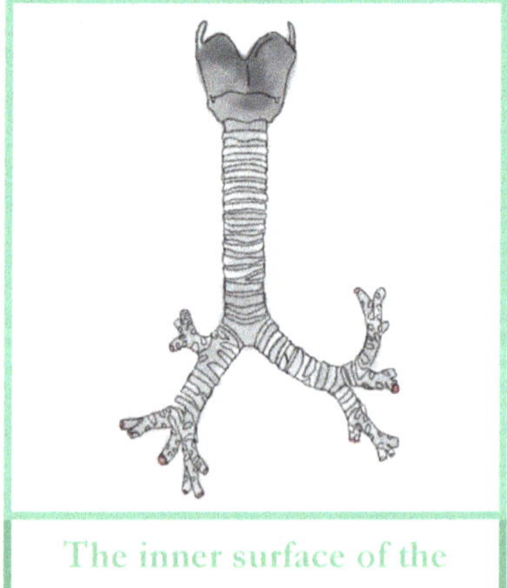

The inner surface of the trachea prevents particles from entering the lungs.

Alveoli are the small, sac-like structures in the lungs where oxygen and carbon dioxide are exchanged, essential to breathing. Their function can be linked to Aeolus, the Greek god in charge of the winds. According to myth, Aeolus lived on the floating island of Aeolia, a place where he kept the four winds under his control. In Virgil's Aeneid, Aeolus is called upon by the goddess Hera to unleash fierce gusts and storms against the Trojan hero Aeneas. At her behest, Aeolus opens the gates of his wind-filled caves, sending turbulent weather to buffet Aeneas's fleet, scattering the ships across the sea.

Much like Aeolus's careful stewardship of the winds, the alveoli manage the flow of air within our bodies. They ensure oxygen is absorbed into the bloodstream and carbon dioxide is released, maintaining a stable balance that keeps us alive. If the alveoli become obstructed or damaged, for example through illness or injury, our ability to breathe properly is compromised, just as the voyage of Aeneas was by Aeolus' unleashed winds.

Digestive System

The digestive system is a series of organs and glands that work together to break down food, absorb nutrients, and eliminate waste from the body.

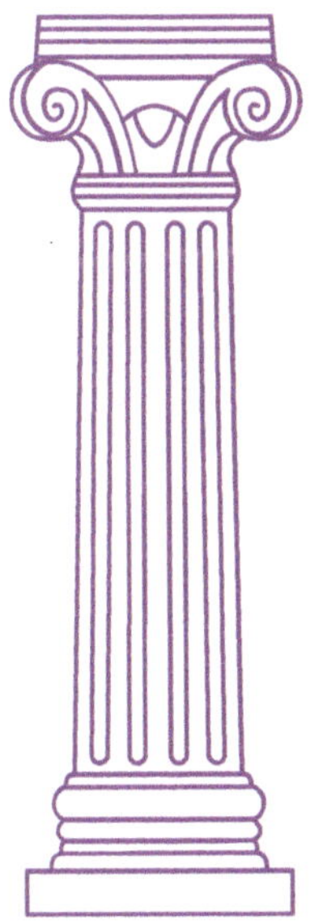

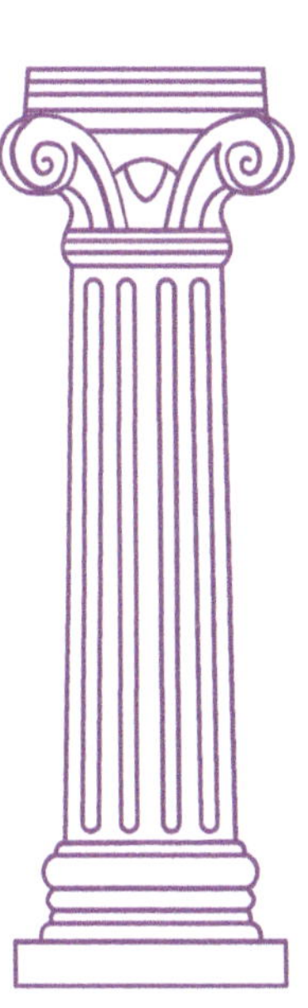

Examples

1. Esophagus

2. Bile Duct

3. Large Intestine

4. Stomach

5. Pancreas

Absorption

sorbere - to suck in

the process by which nutrients from food are taken into the body's bloodstream from the digestive tract

Appendix

pendere - to hang

a small, tube-like structure hanging from the cecum

Bolus

bolus - lump, ball

a mass of chewed food ready to be swallowed

Buccal

bucca - cheek

relating to the cheek or the inside of the mouth

Cecum

caecus - blind, hidden

the beginning of the large intestine; a pouch connected to the junction of the small and large intestines

Other Related Terms

sorbent (*sorbere*)

expend (*pendere*)

pending (*pendere*)

suspend (*pendere*)

buckle (*bucca*)

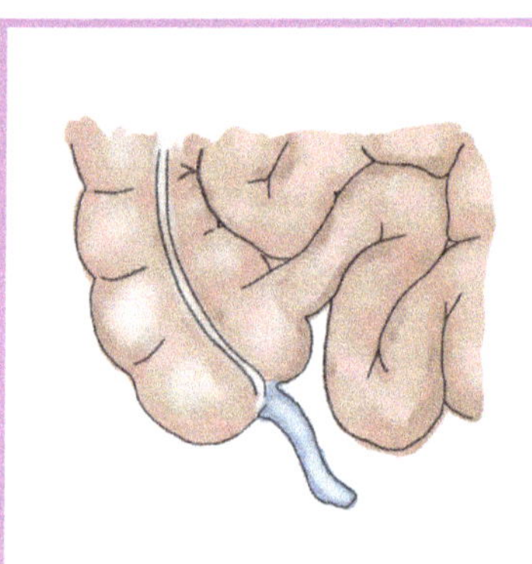

The appendix, once thought to be useless, may play a role in immune function.

Colon

colon - part of a line of verse, fragment

also known as the large intestine and is involved in water absorption and feces formation

Deglutition

glutire - to swallow

the act or process of swallowing

Digestion

digerere - to divide, arrange

the process by which food is broken down into smaller components for absorption

Duodenum

duodeni - twelve each (refers to its length of 12 fingers)

the first part of the small intestine, where most chemical digestion occurs

Gastric

gastricus - stomach, belly (From Greek gaster)

relating to the stomach

Other Related Terms

gluttony (*glutire*)

gesture (*glutire*)

register (*digerere*)

inaugurate (*digerere*)

duodecade (*duodeni*)

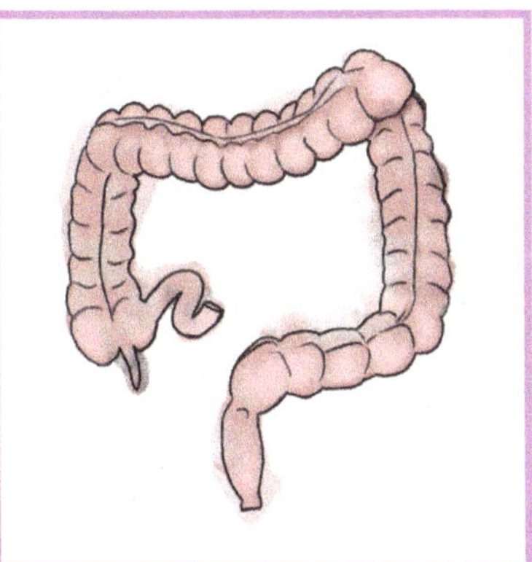

Around 100 trillion microbes live in the colon.

Ileum

ilium - groin, flank

the third and final part of the small intestine, responsible for absorbing nutrients

Intestine

interus - inward, internal

the tubular part of the digestive system that extends from the stomach to the anus

Jejunum

ieiunus - empty (refers to how it was usually found empty during dissections)

the second part of the small intestine, primarily involved in nutrient absorption

Lacteal

lac - milk

lymphatic vessels in the small intestine that absorb dietary fats

Masticate

masticare - to chew

to chew food

Other Related Terms
jade (*ilium*)
intimate (*interus*)
intron (*interus*)
lactose (*lac*)
masticabile (*masticare*)

The human jaws can exert up to 200 pounds of pressure on food during mastication.

Mesentery

mesenterium - middle of the intestine (From Greek mesos)

a fold of tissue that attaches the intestines to the posterior abdominal wall

Nausea

nausea - seasickness

a sensation of unease and discomfort in the stomach

Omentum

omnium - of all things

a fold of peritoneum connecting the stomach with other abdominal organs

Pancreas

pancreas - entirely flesh (From Greek pankreas)

an organ that produces digestive enzymes and hormones like insulin

Pylorus

pyloros - gatekeeper (From Greek pyloros)

the opening from the stomach into the duodenum

Other Related Terms
nautical (*nausea*)
bus (*omnium*)
omnilateral (*omnium*)
omnipotent (*omnium*)
omnivore (*omnium*)

The pancreas produces 1.5 liters of digestive enzymes daily.

Digestive System

Rugae

ruga - wrinkle in the face

folds or wrinkles in the stomach lining that allow for expansion

Saliva

saliva - spittle

the watery fluid produced by salivary glands that aids in digestion

Sphincter

sphincter - band, tightener

a ring-like muscle that controls the passage of substances

Stomach

stomachus - throat, gullet

the organ in which digestion begins

Vomiting

vomere - to puke, spew forth

the forceful expulsion of stomach contents through the mouth

Other Related Terms
corrugate (*ruga*)
rugosity (*ruga*)
salivary (*saliva*)
sphinx (*sphincter*)
vomitory (*vomere*)

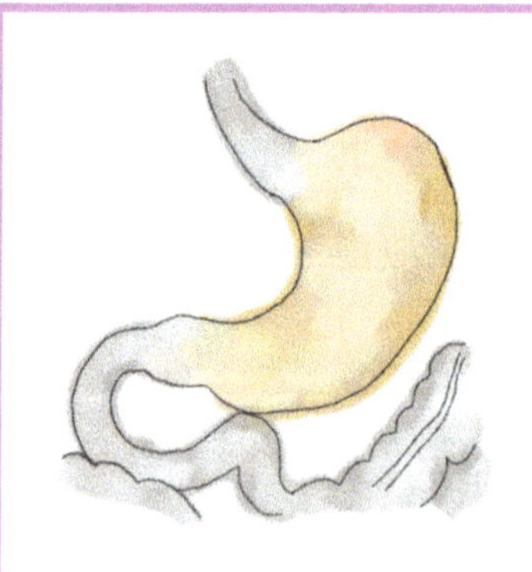

The stomach signals the brain to increase appetite when it is empty.

In the human body, the liver is a vital organ responsible for detoxification, protein synthesis, and the production of biochemicals necessary for digestion. Its regenerative capacity is unparalleled in the human body, allowing it to recover even when a significant portion is damaged or removed. The regenerative capacity of the liver is reflected in the story of Prometheus, the helper of mankind.

Prometheus, a Titan who sided with the gods in

the Titanomachy, is best known in mythology for his defiance of Zeus, the king of the gods. Prometheus had great compassion for humanity. Seeing them struggling in the dark and cold conditions of the world, he secretly stole fire from the gods and gave it to mankind, enabling them to cook food, forge tools, and light their homes. This act of defiance enraged Zeus, who saw it as a challenge to his authority.

As punishment, Zeus devised a cruel fate for Prometheus. He was bound to a rock in the Caucasus Mountains, where each day an eagle (Zeus' sacred bird) would descend to feast on his liver. Each night, however, Prometheus' liver would regenerate, only for the eagle to return the following day and repeat the torment. This cycle of destruction and renewal continued endlessly. In this way, the liver's remarkable resilience mirrors the myth of Prometheus. Just as his liver grew back every night, the human liver has the capacity to heal itself.

Reproductive System

The reproductive system is a collection of internal and external organs in both males and females that work together for the purpose of procreation.

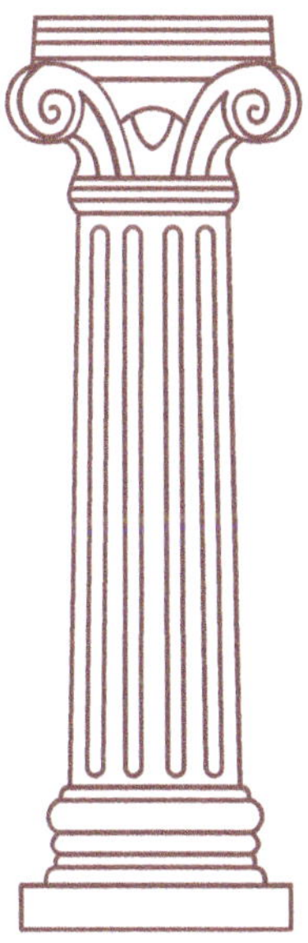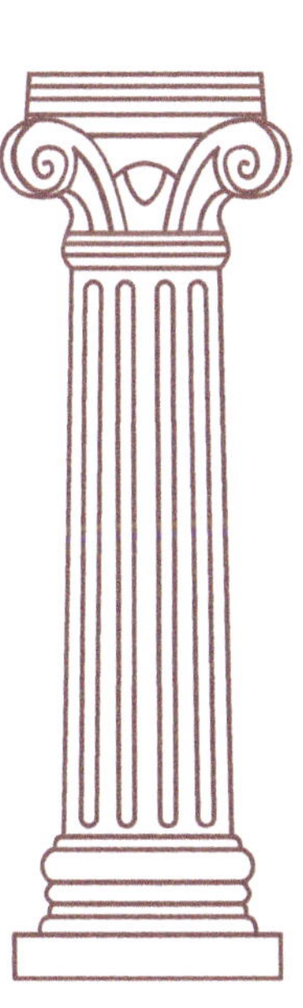

Examples

1. Ovaries

2. Testicles

3. Fallopian Tubes

4. Uterus

5. Urethra

Reproductive System

Amnion

amnion - membrane around a fetus (From Greek amnion)

the membrane surrounding a fetus that forms a fluid-filled sac

Fetus

fetus - pregnancy, offspring

the developing offspring within the uterus from the end of the embryonic stage until birth

Gestation

gerere - to carry, bear

the period of time between conception and birth during which a fetus develops in the uterus

Gland

glans - acorn, nut

an organ that produces and releases substances such as hormones or enzymes

Ovary

ovum - egg

the female reproductive organ that produces eggs and hormones

Other Related Terms
fawn (*fetus*)
congestion (*gerere*)
exaggerate (*gerere*)
oval (*ovum*)
ovulate (*ovum*)

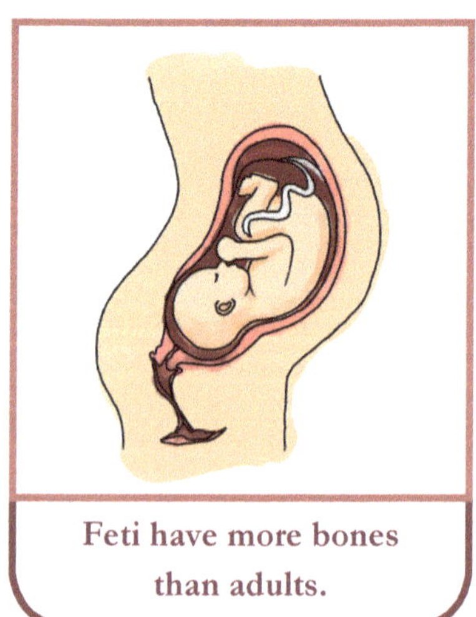

Feti have more bones than adults.

Reproductive System

Prenatal

prae - before + natus - born

relating to the period before birth

Prostate

prostata - leader, one standing in front (From Greek prostates)

a gland in males that surrounds the urethra and produces seminal fluid

Puberty

pubes - adult, manhood

the stage of development when a person becomes capable of reproduction

Scrotum

scrotum - skin, hide

the pouch of skin that contains the testicles

Sperm

sperma - seed (From Greek sperma)

the male reproductive cell

Other Related Terms
innate (*natus*)
nationality (*natus*)
native (*natus*)
pregnant (*natus*)
pubic (*pubes*)

During puberty, voice cracks happen due to growth of the larynx.

Testicle

testis - witness, testicle

the male reproductive organ that produces sperm and hormones

Umbilical

umbilicus - navel

relating to the umbilical cord connecting a fetus to the placenta

Urethra

urethra - passage for urine (From Greek ourethra)

the tube that carries urine and also semen in males

Uterus

uterus - womb, belly

the organ in females where a fetus develops during pregnancy

Vas Deferens

vas - vessel + deferre - to carry away

the duct that carries sperm from the testicle to the urethra

Other Related Terms
detest (*testis*)
protest (*testis*)
testify (*testis*)
defer (*deferre*)
different (*deferre*)

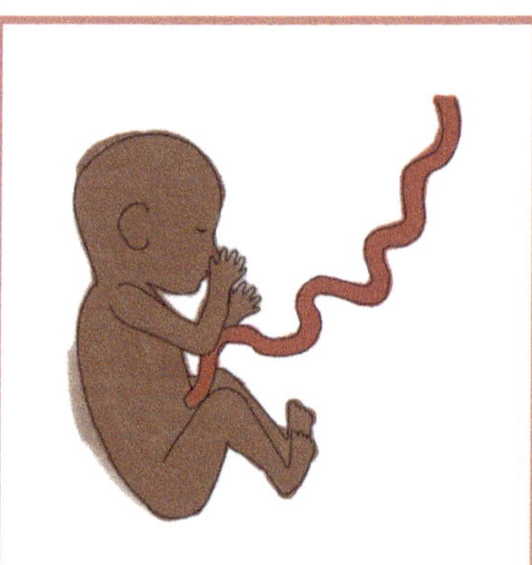

The navel (belly button) is where the umbilical cord attaches.

In ancient Greek tradition, Delphi was considered the physical and spiritual center of the world. According to myth, Zeus set free two eagles from opposite ends of the earth to locate its midpoint. Their paths crossed above a rugged mountainside in central Greece, and the spot where they met became known as Delphi. A sacred stone called the Omphalos, meaning "navel," was placed there to mark this special place.

Delphi's reputation rested on its role as a connection between humans and the gods. It was home to the Oracle of Apollo, the priestess called the Pythia, from whom mortals sought guidance on everything from personal decisions to political affairs. Kings, warriors, and ordinary citizens alike would journey to Delphi for such counsel.

One well-known tale involves Croesus, the wealthy king of Lydia. Before waging war against the Persians, Croesus sought the oracle's advice. The Pythia offered a famously cryptic prophecy: if Croesus crossed the Halys River, he would "destroy a great empire." Interpreting this as a sign he would triumph, Croesus proceeded with the attack, only to find that the great empire destroyed was his own. Stories like this added to the integrity and reputation of Delphi. The ambiguous nature of its prophecies allowed for multiple interpretations and gave the site a sense of divine-like authority.

Other Systems

The immune system defends the body by detecting and eliminating harmful pathogens.

The endocrine system produces and releases hormones that regulate essential bodily processes.

The sensory system gathers information from the environment.

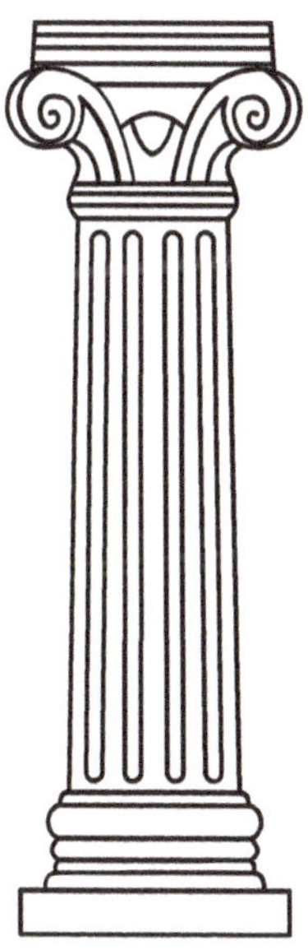

Examples

1. Virus (Immune)

2. Insulin (Endocrine)

3. Vision (Sensory)

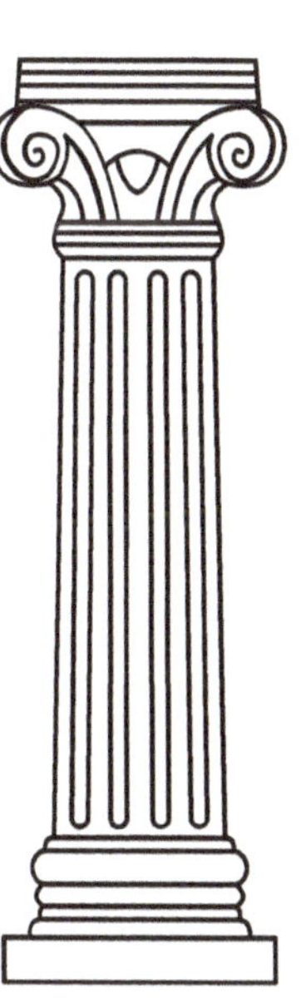

Adjuvant

iuvare - to help

enhances the body's immune response to an antigen

Immunosuppression

immunis - exempt, not paying a share + supprimere - to press down

reduction of the activation or efficacy of the immune system

Infection

inficere - to spoil, stain

invasion and multiplication of harmful microorganisms in the body

Vaccine

vacca - cow (refers to cowpox)

a substance used to stimulate the production of antibodies and provide immunity

Virus

virus - poison, slimy liquid

a small infectious agent that replicates inside living cells

Other Related Terms
aid (*iuvare*)
communion (*immunis*)
pressure (*supprimere*)
defeat (*inficere*)
perfect (*inficere*)

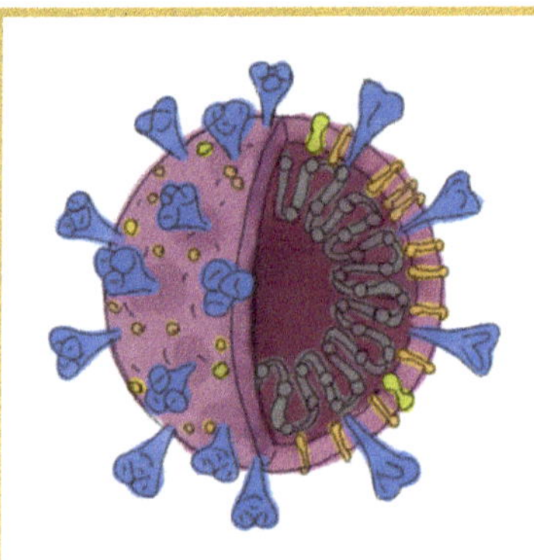

Viruses are considered to be in-between living and nonliving.

Adrenal

ad - to + renes - kidneys

related to the adrenal glands
located near the kidneys

Cortisol

corium - skin

a hormone produced by the
adrenal cortex that helps
regulate metabolism, immune
response, and stress

Insulin

insula - island

a hormone produced by the
pancreas that helps regulate
blood glucose levels by
facilitating the uptake of
glucose into tissues

Pineal

pinus - pine tree

pertaining to the pineal gland, a
small endocrine gland in the
brain

Progesterone

pro - before + gerere - to carry

a hormone produced by the
ovaries and placenta that plays a
role in maintaining pregnancy

Other Related Terms

adrenaline (*renes*)

cortex (*corium*)

peninsula (*insula*)

insulated (*insula*)

suggest (*gerere*)

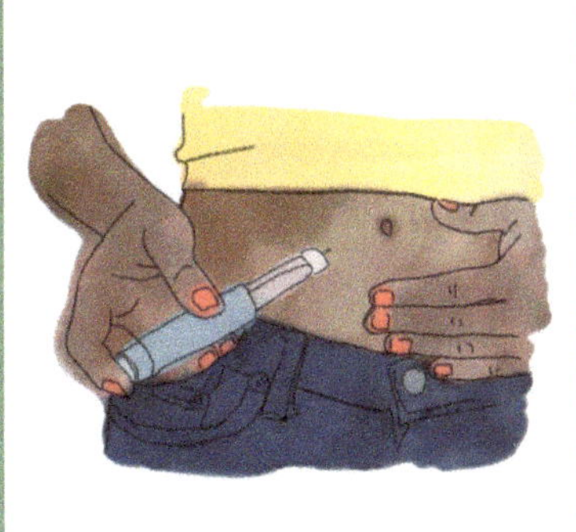

The first insulin treatments
for humans came from cows
and pigs.

Auditory

audire - to hear

the sense of hearing and the organs involved in detecting sound

Gustatory

gustare - to taste

related to the sense of taste and the perception of flavors

Ocular

oculus - eye

related to the eyes and the sense of vision

Perception

percepire - to perceive

the process by which sensory information is interpreted and understood by the brain

Tactile

tangere - to touch

involving the sense of touch and the ability to feel physical sensations

Other Related Terms
audience (*audire*)
disgust (*gustare*)
binocular (*oculus*)
capable (*percepire*)
contagious (*tangere*)

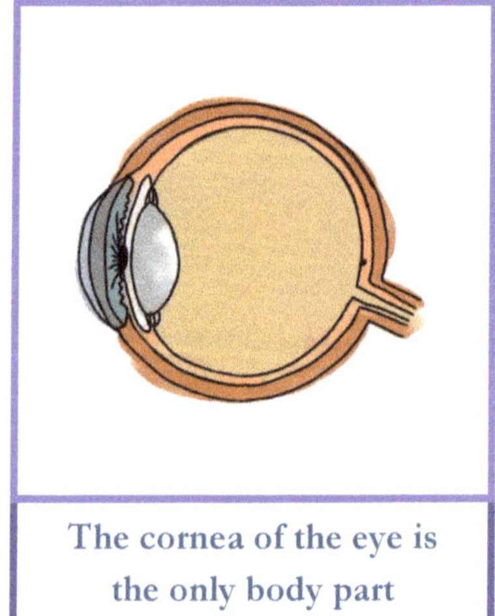

The cornea of the eye is the only body part without blood vessels.

Medusa is one of Greek mythology's most recognized figures. She is known for her gaze, which could turn those who looked upon her to stone. This lethal power targets an individual's sight, an ability that is both a gift and a vulnerability. In the human body, this sight comes from our eyes, serving as the primary channel through which we perceive the world.

According to the Roman poet Ovid, Medusa was originally a beautiful maiden serving as a priestess in Athena's temple. However, when she was caught being seduced by Poseidon, Athena became enraged and transformed Medusa's hair into writhing serpents. From then on, anyone whose eyes met Medusa's gaze would immediately turn to stone.

The most famous account of Medusa involves the hero Perseus, a son of Zeus. Tasked with bringing back her head, Perseus avoided looking directly at her by using a polished shield as a mirror. By doing so, he escaped her petrifying gaze and successfully slew her. When he severed her head, the blood that spilled onto the earth gave rise to two offspring: the winged horse Pegasus and the warrior Chrysaor.

However, Medusa's head retained its power even after her death. Later, Perseus encountered the Titan Atlas on his journey home. Atlas, who bore the weight of the sky upon his shoulders, refused Perseus shelter in his lands, fearing a prophecy that a son of Zeus would steal golden apples from his orchard. Angered by this inhospitable reception, Perseus unveiled the severed head of Medusa. The Titan gazed upon it and was transformed into the Atlas mountains.

List of Terms

Abductor (Latin: *abducere* - to lead away)

Absorption (Latin: *sorbere* - to suck in)

Accumbens (Latin: *accumbere* - to recline or lie down)

Adductor (Latin: *adducere* - to lead towards)

Adjuvant (Latin: *iuvare* - to help)

Adrenal (Latin: *ad* - to, near + *renes* - kidneys)

Afferent (Latin: *afferre* - to carry towards)

Albinism (Latin: *albus* - white)

Alveolar (Latin: *alveolus* - socket, small cavity)

Amnion (Latin: *amnion* - membrane around a fetus)

Angina (Latin: *angere* - to strangle, suffocate)

Apnea (Latin: *apnoea* - absence of breath)

Appendix (Latin: *pendere* - to hang)

Articulation (Latin: *artus* - joint)

Atrium (Latin: *atrium* - first main room of a house)

Auditory (Latin: *audire* - to hear)

Biceps (Latin: *bi* - two + *caput* - head)

Bolus (Latin: *bolus* - lump, ball)

Brachial (Latin: *brachium* - arm)

Brain (Latin: *cerebrum* - brain)

Bronchus (Latin: *bronchus* - wind pipe)

Buccal (Latin: *bucca* - cheek)

Calcaneus (Latin: *calx* - heel)

Callus (Latin: *callum* - hard

Capillary (Latin: *capillus* - hair)

Carbon (Latin: *carbo* - coal)

Cardiac (Latin: *cardiacus* - pertaining to the heart)

Carpal (Latin: *carpus* - wrist)

List of Terms

Cartilage (Latin: *cartilago* - cartilage, gristle)

Cauda Equina (Latin: *cauda* - tail + *equus* - horse)

Cecum (Latin: *caecus* - blind, hidden)

Cervical (Latin: *cervix* - neck)

Cilia (Latin: *cilium* - eyelash)

Circulation (Latin: *circulus* - circle, small ring)

Cisterna (Latin: *cista* - chest, box)

Clavicle (Latin: *clavis* - key, bolt)

Collagen (Latin: *colla* - glue)

Colon (Latin: *colon* - part of a verse, fragment)

Congestion (Latin: *cum* - with + *gerere* - to carry, bring, pile up)

Contusion (Latin: *tundere* - to beat, strike)

Coronary (Latin: *corona* - crown, wreath)

Corpus Callosum (Latin: *corpus* - body + *callus* - hard, tough)

Cortisol (Latin: *corium* - skin)

Cranium (Latin: *cranium* - skull)

Cutaneous (Latin: *cutis* - skin)

Cyanosis (Latin: *cyanosis* - dark blue)

Deglutition (Latin: *glutire* - to swallow)

Dermatologist (Latin: *derma* - skin)

Diaphragm (Latin: *diaphragma* - partition, barrier)

Digestion (Latin: *digerere* - to divide, arrange)

Dorsal (Latin: *dorsum* - back)

Duodenum (Latin: *duodeni* - twelve each)

Edema (Latin: *oedema* - swelling)

Efferent (Latin: *effere* - to carry away)

Erythema (Latin: *erythema* - redness)

Expiration (Latin: *spirare* - to breathe)

Extensor (Latin: *extendere* - to stretch out)

Fetus (Latin: *fetus* - pregnancy, offspring)

Fiber (Latin: *fibra* - leaf, lobe)

Fibrillation (Latin: *fibra* - fiber)

Fibula (Latin: *fibula* - clasp, brooch, peg, pin)

List of Terms

Flexor (Latin: *flectere* - to bend)

Follicle (Latin: *follis* - bag, sac)

Gangrene (Latin: *gangraena* - an eating or gnawing sore)

Gastric (Latin: *gastricus* - stomach, belly)

Gestation (Latin: *gerere* - to carry, bear)

Gland (Latin: *glans* - acorn, nut)

Glia (Latin: *glia* - glue)

Gluteus (Latin: *glutaeus* - buttocks, the rump)

Gustatory (Latin: *gustare* - to taste)

Hippocampus (Latin: *hippocampus* - seahorse)

Humerus (Latin: *umerus* - shoulder)

Humidify (Latin: *humidus* - moist, wet + *facere* - to make)

Hypertension (Latin: *hyper* - over + *tendere* - to stretch)

Ileum (Latin: *ilium* - groin, flank)

Ilium (Latin: *ilium* - flank)

Immunosuppression (Latin: *immunis* - exempt, not paying a share + *supprimere* - to press down)

Impetigo (Latin: *impetus* - an attack)

Impulse (Latin: *impellere* - to push against)

Incision (Latin: *caedere* - to cut)

Infection (Latin: *inficere* - to spoil, stain)

Inflammation (Latin: *flamma* - flame)

Inhalation (Latin: inhalare - to breathe in)

Insulin (Latin: insula - island)

Intercostal (Latin: inter - between + costa - rib)

Intestine (Latin: interus - inward, internal)

Jejunum (Latin: ieiunus - empty)

Joint (Latin: *iunctus* - united, connected, associated)

Laceration (Latin: *lacer* - torn into pieces, mangled)

Lacteal (Latin: *lac* - milk)

Larynx (Latin: *larynx* - upper windpipe)

Latissimus (Latin: *latissimus* - widest)

Lesion (Latin: *laedere* - to strike, hurt, injure)

List of Terms

Limbic (Latin: *limbus* - edge)
Lobe (Latin: *lobus* - hull, pod)
Lumbar (Latin: *lumbus* - loin)
Mandible (Latin: *mandere* - to chew)
Marrow (Latin: *medulla* - marrow)
Masticate (Latin: *masticare* - to chew)
Melanin (Latin: *melas* - a black spot on the skin)
Meninges (Latin: *meninx* - membrane)
Mesentery (Latin: *mesenterium* - middle of the intestine)
Mitral (Latin: *mitra* - headband, turban, bishop's hat)
Motor (Latin: *movere* - to move)
Mucous (Latin: *mucus* - slimy, mucus)
Muscle (Latin: *mus* - mouse)
Myocardium (Latin: *myo* - muscle + *cor* - heart)
Nasal (Latin: *nasus* - nose)
Nausea (Latin: *nausea* - seasickness)
Nebulizer (Latin: *nebula* - mist)
Nodule (Latin: *nodus* - knot)
Nucleus (Latin: *nucleus* - kernel)
Oblique (Latin: *obliquus* - slanting)
Occipital (Latin: *ob* - in the back of + *caput* - head)
Occlusion (Latin: *occludere* - to close up)
Ocular (Latin: *oculus* - eye)
Olfactory (Latin: *olfacere* - to get the smell of)
Omentum (Latin: *omnium* - of all things)
Osseous (Latin: *os* - bone)
Ossification (Latin: *os* - bone + *facere* - to make)
Ovary (Latin: *ovum* - egg)
Pacemaker (Latin: *pax* - peace)
Palate (Latin: *palatum* - roof of the mouth)
Palpitation (Latin: *palpitare* - to throb, flutter)
Pancreas (Latin: *pancreas* - entirely flesh)
Papule (Latin: *papula* - pimple, swelling)

List of Terms

Papule (Latin: *papula* - pimple, swelling)

Parietal (Latin: *paries* - wall)

Patella (Latin: *pateo* - lie open)

Pectoral (Latin: *pectus* - chest)

Pelvis (Latin: *pelvis* - basin, laver)

Perception (Latin: *percepire* - to perceive)

Pineal (Latin: *pinus* - pine tree)

Pleura (Latin: *pleuron* - rib, side)

Plexus (Latin: *plectere* - to twine, braid, fold)

Pons (Latin: *pons* - bridge)

Prenatal (Latin: *prae* - before + *natus* - born)

Progesterone (Latin: *pro* - before + *gerere* - to carry)

Pronation (Latin: *pronare* - to bend forward)

Prostate (Latin: *prostata* - leader, one standing in front)

Pruritus (Latin: *prurire* - to itch)

Puberty (Latin: *pubes* - adult, manhood)

Pulmonary (Latin: *pulmo* - lung)

Pylorus (Latin: *pyloros* - gatekeeper)

Rash (Latin: *rasus* - scrape)

Receptor (Latin: *recipere* - to receive)

Rectus (Latin: *rectus* - straight)

Reflex (Latin: *reflectere* - to bend back)

Rhinitis (Latin: *rhino* - nose)

Rugae (Latin: *ruga* - wrinkle in the face)

Sacrum (Latin: *sacer* - holy. sacred)

Saliva (Latin: *saliva* - spittle)

Sarcomere (Latin: *saro* - flesh)

Scar (Latin: *eschara* - scar)

Scrotum (Latin: *scrotum* - skin, hide)

Sebaceous (Latin: *sebum* - tallow, grease)

Sensory (Latin: *sentire* - to perceive, feel)

Septum (Latin: *saepes* - hedge, fence)

Sinus (Latin: *sinus* - curve, fold)

List of Terms

Skeletal (Latin: *sceletus* - skeleton)

Soleus (Latin: *solea* - sole)

Spasm (Latin: *spasmus* - a spasm)

Sperm (Latin: *sperma*- seed)

Sphincter (Latin: *sphincter* - band, tightener)

Spinal (Latin: *spina* - backbone, thorn)

Sputum (Latin: *spuere* - to spit)

Stenosis (Latin: *stenosis* - a narrowing)

Stomach (Latin: *stomachus* - throat, gullet)

Suture (Latin: *suere* - to sew)

Tachycardia (Latin: *tachy* - swift + *cor* - heart)

Tactile (Latin: *tangere* - to touch)

Talus (Latin: *talus* - heel)

Temporal (Latin: *tempus* - time, season)

Tendon (Latin: *tendere* - to stretch)

Teres (Latin: *terere* - to rub)

Testicle (Latin: *testis* - witness, testicle)

Tetanus (Latin *tetanus* - spasm)

Tibia (Latin: *tibia* - shinbone, pipe, flute)

Torso (Latin: *thyrsus* - stalk, stem)

Trachea (Latin: *trachia* - windpipe)

Tricuspid (Latin: *tri* - three + *cuspis* - point)

Ulcer (Latin: *ulcus* - sore)

Umbilical (Latin: *umbilicus* - navel)

Urethra (Latin: *urethra* - passage for urine)

Uterus (Latin: *uterus* - womb, belly)

Vaccine (Latin: *vacca* - cow) (refers to cowpox)

Vagus (Latin: *vagus* - wandering, straying)

Valve (Latin: *valva* - section of folding or revolving door)

Varicose (Latin: *varix* - dilated vein)

Vas Deferens (Latin: *vas* - vessel + *deferre* to carry away)

Vascular (Latin: *vasculum* - small vessel)

Vasoconstriction (Latin: *vas* - vessel + *constringere* - to bind together)

List of Terms

Vasodilation (Latin: *vas* - vessel + *dis* - apart + *latus* wide)

Vastus (Latin: *vastus* - huge)

Vena Cava (Latin: *vena* - vein + *cavus* - hollow)

Venous (Latin: *vena* - vein)

Ventilation (Latin: *ventus* - wind)

Ventricle (Latin: *venter* - belly)

Vertebra (Latin: *vertere* - to turn)

Vessel (Latin: *vas* - vessel)

Virus (Latin: *virus* - poison, slimy liquid)

Visceral (Latin: *viscus* - internal organ/part of the body)

Vitiligo (Latin: *vitiligo* - blemish)

Voice (Latin: *vox* - voice)

Vomiting (Latin: *vomere* - to puke, spew forth)

Zygomatic (Latin: *zygomaticus* - pertaining to the zygoma)

Eshaan Vasudev

Eshaan Vasudev is a high school student at the University School of Milwaukee. He was introduced to Latin and the classics in his freshman year of high school, and since then has been very passionate about studying the ancient world. He is very involved in medical research on a variety of topics related to COVID-19, esophageal cancer, and heart disease.

Krish Vasudev

Krish Vasudev is an undergraduate student at the Washington University in St. Louis. He started learning Latin in middle school. His interests span from playing the violin, volunteering for various organizations and playing soccer. He has been involved in medical research related to COVID-19, liver transplantation, neurosurgery and xenotransplantation.

Ron Roessler is a board-certified emergency medicine physician with over 20 years of experience. He has also been studying, teaching, and coaching Latin for over four decades, blending his expertise in both fields. *Arbor Medicinae*, co-authored with his students Krish and Eshaan, combines this unique background to explore the ancient roots of medical terminology, making it a valuable resource for students, patients, and pre-med professionals alike.

Aida El-Hajjar

Aida El-Hajjar is a high school student at the University School of Milwaukee, with a passion for classics, science, and art. She began creating art during the pandemic and now enjoys combining it with her other interests. Aida plans to pursue a career as a psychiatrist as well as continuing to pursue the arts in the future.

Fifty percent of the proceeds from the sale of this book will be donated to Wisconsin Junior Classical League (WJCL), National Junior Classical League (NJCL) and to promote Latin education.